The Art of Letting Go

The Journey from Separation in Love to Fulfillment in Life

Published by
Carlino & Company
Honolulu, Hawaii

New Edition

Copyright 2000 Carlino Giampolo

All Rights Reserved.

This book may not be reproduced in whole or in part, except by written permission from the publisher.

ISBN: 0-937827-05-3

First Printing June 2000

Second Printing August 2000

Visit our Web site at: http://www.theartoflettinggo.com

Design, typography and print production by
Blaine Fergerstrom, ZZ-Type, Honolulu, Hawaii

This book is dedicated to all those people who are now in transition between the painful breakup of an intimate relationship and the joy of new beginnings. It is not meant as an authoritative guide for living; rather, it represents the sharing of the author's personal experience. May the readers find a source of inspiration in the pages that follow and the means necessary for their own liberation.

My deepest gratitude to Dr. James Cascaito
for help in the final writing of the text.

Contents

Introduction

Your pain is the breaking of the shell
that encloses your understanding.

Kahlil Gibran

Letting go of a loved one means moving from a period of relative security into one which demands the redefining of an individual's place and purpose in life. This is a painful yet necessary process. The transition involves coming to terms with two dimensions of challenge: the private reevaluation of self and the mode of interacting with others. In the private realm, an individual reflects upon the nature of personal resources with which to live through the suffering involved in separation. Once a healthy attitude toward the situation has been established, the stage is set for embracing daily experiences with the confidence and strength upon which a meaningful life can be built.

The confusion which accompanies the pain of a separation is one of the main impediments to resolving the dilemma of people in the process of letting go of a loved one. This confusion is, of course, characterized by unique circumstances, which relate to individual situations. The essence of the experience of separation is, however, universal. What follows on these pages is a journey through those areas of concern which all separations have in common. The reader's sincere reflection upon those realities which touch on all love separations can provide what is needed for every individual's liberation.

Introduction

Why did you enter into the relationship with the person from whom you are now separating?

_____

_____

_____

_____

What did you expect to get from the relationship?

_____

_____

_____

_____

What is the specific pain you are feeling now?

_____

_____

_____

Is that pain related to what you expected to get from the relationship?

_____

_____

_____

What do you want in your life now?

_____

_____

_____

_____

3

Do you honestly expect to let go of all the negativity surrounding your breakup?

_____

_____

_____

How would you describe your desire to let go?

_____

_____

_____

Should your desire to let go weaken, what steps will you take to strengthen your desire?

_____

_____

_____

On a piece of paper write the following affirmation and place it where you can see it often.

I am willing to let go.

Relax, and for 10 minutes reflect on what it would be like to let go completely. Record your thoughts and feelings.

_____

_____

_____

_____

_____

_____

Love

The falling out of lovers
is the renewing of love.

Robert Burton

Surround yourself with love. Though this may seem
to you the most impossible emotion to experience in
the first stages following a separation, it is to become
your course of action when you realize that love is the
key to your control of self and to the door that is opening toward your new reality. Love is what brought you
into your relationship and love is the power that will
lead you to the meaningful resolution of your situation.

This decision to love must first take effect with reference to yourself and to the person from whom you are
separating. You must love yourself for those qualities
which brought you into the realm of that other person:
your willingness to give of yourself and to take the risk
of being hurt. And to love the other person in spite of
the pain you are feeling is to allow that person the same
freedom you will both need in order to move on. Love is
a force that renews us and prepares us for tomorrow.
Hatred is a shackle that keeps us tied to the past. Drop
the shackles!

The one from whom you have separated will not soon
be forgotten, though great distances may separate the

two of you. Give the memory of that person the chance to help you by insisting on remembering the beautiful experiences that united you. The painful ones which separated you will need no coaxing from the memory. Turn your anger into love. Take the qualities you found in the other person and develop them in yourself, use them as a way of better experiencing your love for all the others who are important in your life. After all, those were qualities which brought you into love and they are no less worthy today.

Love has no guilt and no boundaries. In fact, it has no definition. Yes, it is the force which takes us out of ourselves so that we may share ourselves with others. Yet it is also the force that leads us into ourselves, so that we may understand and prepare ourselves for the act of giving. You cannot resolve the bitterness and pain of the separation you are experiencing by continuing to dwell on these feelings. Come alive with the force which is the essence of life itself. You are leaving one relationship, one stop in your journey. There is still a path before you. Walk in love.

Love

How would you describe self-love?

_____

_____

_____

_____

How would you describe unconditional love?

_____

_____

_____

_____

Was your relationship one of unconditional love?

_____

_____

_____

_____

Why do you deserve to be loved?

_____

_____

_____

_____

What are some of the qualities of a loving person?

_____

_____

_____

_____

Which one of those qualities do you want to put into action today?

_____

_____

_____

What negative beliefs do you have about love that you want to change?

_____

_____

_____

_____

In what different areas of your life can you express the love you have?

_____

_____

_____

_____

Relax, and for 10 minutes feel total self-love. Record your thoughts and feelings.

_____

_____

_____

_____

_____

_____

_____

Spiritual Power

Oh! there is never sorrow of heart
That shall lack a timely end,
If but to God we turn, and ask
Of Him to be our friend!

William Wordsworth

Every human relationship leads us to a deeper consciousness of what lies beyond this earthly existence. All too frequently we forget this. Sometimes it takes an experience like the one you are now going through to enable you to place human events in their proper perspective. While it is true that much is to be gained by turning to other human beings in our time of need, we all feel the necessity of having recourse to a Power greater than ourselves. This Power is called God/ Goddess/All That Is by some, and for some it has no name, it simply is!

Pray to this Higher Force. Prayer means opening oneself to a channel of communication with the Power that lies beyond us. It means talking to that Power, giving thanks for our blessings, accepting our trials, admitting our weaknesses and asking for comfort and assurance. It is easy to see that the act of prayer, the act of openly coming to terms with ourselves by placing our doubts and confusion into the hands of some Force greater than ourselves, is part of the act of love itself. Thus, by praying we renew our confidence in love, which is the focal point of our human existence.

Clear your mind. Relax your body. Open yourself to yourself and speak out from your heart to this Higher Force. This is prayer. You need not formulate into words what you wish to express. Your willingness to communicate your feelings is a language in itself. Then listen. This is meditation. The two acts of prayer and meditation should accompany one another. What you hear will be a form of silence. A divine silence. A comforting from afar.

Let the fruit of this act of communication be the sustenance of your daily life. You will begin to function more effectively in your world, the world which stares at you face to face, after you have undergone a painful separation, if you will just place some of the pain and confusion in the hands of that Power which is capable of assuming the suffering of all mankind. By binding yourself spiritually to that Power which binds all humans together, you reinforce your belief in your own ability to continue your quest for meaningful human relationships. The burdens of the daily life you are now facing will seem lighter for you. This will make you stronger for the work which lies ahead of you.

Spiritual Power

Describe your spiritual relationship with a
Higher Power.

_____

_____

_____

_____

_____

What can you do to add depth to that relationship?

_____

_____

_____

_____

How would you describe your soul?

_____

_____

_____

_____

In what ways does your soul communicate to you?

_____

_____

_____

_____

What else comprises your spiritual world?

_____

_____

_____

_____

Think of one positive experience from the past which occurred when you placed your pain and confusion in the hands of a Higher Power?

_____

_____

_____

_____

Describe your positive feelings concerning that experience.

_____

_____

_____

_____

_____

Relax, and for 10 minutes reflect on the words "Spiritual Power." Record your thoughts and feelings.

_____

_____

_____

_____

_____

_____

Beliefs

Believe that life is worth living,
And your belief will help create the fact.

William James

The measure of success you achieve in the process of letting go will be determined to a great degree by your beliefs. They are the framework upon which you build your future. Your beliefs are the foundation for the shape your life will take from this point onward. As such they must be both solid and flexible. In other words, you must always be sure that the beliefs which form the base of your decisions and actions are strong enough to provide support for the directions in which you are planning to go; and yet at the same time, if these building blocks do not allow for creative self-expansion, then progress will be beyond your reach.

By acknowledging which of your beliefs are beneficial to you right now and which are not, you will achieve two goals; your liberation from the pain of separation and the reconstruction of a healthy base from which to conduct your future course of action.

It is during this time that you must assure yourself that the foundations of your actions are secure and capable of permitting growth and change. Remember that your beliefs predispose you to action; they precede experience. Take this opportunity to challenge your beliefs in all areas of your life. Hold onto those convictions that enable you to maintain a sense of self-worth and allow you to control your own destiny. Change those that you know are preventing or slowing down your progress toward realizing your full potential as a human being.

Focus on where you are now. Analyze those beliefs of yours which have most to do with the process of letting go. Understand that if your beliefs in this process are centered around personal growth and healing, then your thoughts will coincide with these beliefs and will be guided by them. In this way you can actually empower yourself and bring about this growth and healing.

In order to have a more complete understanding of the fundamental beliefs which determine your actions, examine your beliefs with reference to each chapter of this book. By doing so you will be able to identify the underlying beliefs that are hurting yourself and others. Similarly, you will be assured of those basic principles that are essential to your well being and to creating wholesome relationships with other people. And as you make the choice to build upon these positive attitudes, your potential for growth and happiness will expand.

Beliefs

What beliefs of yours about the letting-go process may be preventing you from letting go easily?

_____

_____

_____

_____

Change what you have listed above into positive statements.

_____

_____

_____

_____

What beliefs have successfully guided you through past painful experiences in your life?

_____

_____

_____

_____

In areas of your life other than this relationship, what past beliefs taught to you by family, schools, culture, religion and society would you now want to change?

_____

_____

_____

_____

_____

_____

_____

_____

_____

Write down the new beliefs you want to add to your life.

_____

_____

_____

_____

_____

_____

_____

Relax, and for 10 minutes reflect on the importance of beliefs in your life. Record your thoughts and feelings.

_____

_____

_____

_____

_____

_____

_____

_____

_____

Forgiveness

To err is human, to forgive divine.

Alexander Pope

The road on which you are traveling is not an easy one. Why clutter it with more obstacles than it already presents to you? Tear down the stumbling block of resentment and cast it aside. Forgive! Clear the path and get on with your journey.

It is unrealistic to place all the blame for the events that have led to your separation on the other person. This you already know. And by insisting on continuing your resentment even for those acts which are clearly the fault of the other, you only persist in creating an even more difficult situation for yourself. What good can come from dredging up all of the negative aspects of the other person's character? None. And whether you are willing to admit it or not, the relationship which the two of you formed together was made possible first and foremost by those characteristics which you have in common.

To forgive is to release from blame. You should remember that your act of forgiving, of removing the blame, should be two-fold: to forgive yourself and to also forgive the other person.

Forgive the other person, so that you may both be able to see the world clearly in the present tense. Blame, like hatred, keeps you a prisoner of the past. You have your version of that past. The other person has another version. You both have done what you were able to do with the resources at your disposal! That is all history. Close that book!

Forgive yourself for any shortcomings in your part of the relationship. This is one of the most important keys to self-respect. Release yourself from guilt. Pardon yourself as you pardon the other person. Just as you were capable of committing some of the errors that led to the decline of the relationship, you are also worthy of forgiveness. This pardon may or may not come from the other person. Most importantly it must come from you. You are in a position now where you need to concentrate most of your energies in the direction of rebuilding that confidence which is the first step to rebuilding your life.

Your future relationships, starting from today, will bear the stamp of your self-respect as it is today. By eliminating that which is of no value to you, namely the useless blame of yourself or others, you are ready to face the future now.

Forgiveness *(Yourself)*

These two pages are intended to help you in the process of forgiving yourself. The next two pages are meant to assist you in forgiving the person from whom you are separating. And the following two pages, if necessary, will guide you in forgiving a third person involved in the relationship.

For what specifically do you want to forgive yourself in reference to this breakup?

_____

Are you resisting forgiving yourself? Do you view forgiving yourself as weakness?

_____

Do you fear the act of forgiving?

_____

In forgiving yourself, something dies emotionally. What is this "something" for you?

_____

Go through the grieving process.

What are you denying?

_____

What are you refusing to accept?

_____

What are you angry about?

_____

What are you feeling guilty about?

_____

Whom are you blaming?

_____

Are you feeling depressed?

_____

What are you going to do about your grief?

_____

Are you feeling self-pity?

_____

Are you feeling a sense of self-righteousness?

_____

Did you either cause or allow this situation to occur?

_____

How will your life be different when you forgive yourself?

_____

What do you want to have as a physical symbol of forgiving yourself?

_____

Create your own meditation and forgive yourself.

Relax, and for 10 minutes reflect on the new positive emotions which result from forgiving yourself. Record your thoughts and feelings.

_____

_____

_____

_____

Forgiveness *(The person from whom you are separating)*

For what specifically do you want to forgive the person from whom you are separating?

_____

Are you resisting forgiving that person? Do you view forgiving that person as weakness?

_____

Do you fear the act of forgiving?

_____

In forgiving the person from whom you are separating, something dies emotionally. What is this "something" for you?

_____

Go through the grieving process.

What are you denying?

_____

What are you refusing to accept?

_____

What are you angry about?

_____

What are you feeling guilty about?

_____

Whom are you blaming?

_____

Are you feeling depressed?

_____

What are you going to do about your grief?

_____

Are you feeling self-pity?

_____

Are you feeling a sense of self-righteousness?

_____

Did you either cause or allow this situation to occur?

_____

How will your life be different when you forgive the person from whom you are separating?

_____

What do you want to have as a physical symbol of forgiving that person?

_____

Create your own meditation and forgive that person.

Relax, and for 10 minutes reflect on the new positive emotions which result from forgiving the person from whom you are separating. Record your thoughts and feelings.

_____

_____

_____

_____

_____

Forgiveness *(A third person, if necessary)*

For what specifically do you want to forgive this third person?

_____

Are you resisting forgiving this third person?

_____

Do you view forgiving this person as weakness?

_____

Do you fear the act of forgiving?

_____

In forgiving this third person, something dies emotionally. What is this "something" for you?

_____

Go through the grieving process.

_____

What are you denying?

_____

What are you refusing to accept?

_____

What are you angry about?

_____

What are you feeling guilty about?

_____

Whom are you blaming?

_____

Are you feeling depressed?

What are you going to do about your grief?

Are you feeling self-pity?

Are you feeling a sense of self-righteousness?

Did you either cause or allow this situation to occur?

How will your life be different when you forgive this third person?

What do you want to have as a physical symbol of forgiving this third person?

Create your own meditation and forgive this third person.

Relax, and for 10 minutes reflect on the new positive emotions which result from forgiving this third person. Record your thoughts and feelings.

Trust

Better trust all, and be deceived
And weep that trust and that deceiving
Than doubt one heart that if believed
Had blessed one's life with true believing.

Frances Anne Kemble

Begin now to open yourself to others. Do not put this off. Trust in the world, though it may seem hostile. This will be perhaps one of the most difficult tasks for you to accomplish in the weeks and months that lie ahead of you. Embrace the task willingly, using as your primary tool the awareness you have of the good you have received from all those who love you.

Your initial response to a painful separation may include an intense reluctance to place your trust in someone once again. You can overcome this hesitation by concentrating on the relationship between the various forms of love and affection which surround us in our lives. Just as you can count on the tenderness and sincerity of some friends and family members, you can count on the possibility of this love from others as well. To transfer the negative feelings which you may associate with the relationship you are ending to the world at large is unrealistic.

Every situation is unique. Every person is unique. Think of how you first met one of your good friends, perhaps years ago, quite by accident. Think of how this friendship grew stronger through the years, battling all adversity. You and that one person have maintained the love of friendship through your trust in one another. Perhaps other friendships were not so successful. In the same way you must open yourself to the possibility of entering into an intimate relationship which will go beyond the one which you have just left. Do not go out in haste in search of such a relationship. But do not shut yourself off from the possibility of growing into a close human bond once again.

In order to prepare yourself for this stage of opening up to new relationships, trust in yourself. Be honest with yourself.

Those qualities which are a permanent part of your character and which have led you into meaningful interactions with all those you have ever loved and who have loved you did not suddenly vanish when this relationship came to an end. Your ability to open up to others has not disappeared. Your potential for loving, in spite of the risks involved, always was and still is the main source of your faith in life. Renew this faith by trusting the world once again. Renew your life by maintaining trust in yourself.

Trust

Describe one positive past experience that resulted when you trusted yourself.

_____

_____

_____

_____

What are some obstacles blocking you from trusting someone again in an intimate relationship?

_____

_____

_____

In what ways were you betrayed by the person from whom you are now separating?

_____

_____

_____

_____

How do you feel about that betrayal?

_____

_____

_____

_____

In what ways may you have betrayed the person from whom you are now separating? If you do not believe you have betrayed the other person, in what other past experience may you have betrayed another?

_____

_____

_____

_____

How do you feel about that betrayal?

_____

_____

_____

_____

Are you beginning to compare other people to the person from whom you are now separating?

_____

_____

_____

Relax, and for 10 minutes reflect on the importance of continuing to trust yourself and others. Record your thoughts and feelings.

_____

_____

_____

_____

_____

_____

Self-Image

The great mystery is not that we should have
been thrown down here at random between
the profusion of matter and that of the stars;
it is that from our very prison we should
draw, from our own selves, images powerful
enough to deny our nothingness.

André Malraux

The way in which you see yourself and your relationship to the world around you is the core of the
image you convey to your fellow human beings, and lies
at the center of the interactions which take place
between you and them. Before you can hope to succeed
in achieving harmony with the world, you must first
confront the task of understanding yourself. This is of
course, an on-going process, one in which you have been
constantly involved throughout your life. During this
period of your separation from a loved one, however, it
is absolutely essential that you concentrate on the
importance of self-knowledge. The primary energies
necessary for your victory over this present crisis can
come only from you.

Maintain your self-respect and your sense of self-
worth. Your positive qualities and achievements in life to

this point have not suddenly dropped out of existence. The awareness you have of your own capacity for working through difficult situations is a priceless treasure at this time. Use it to its fullest advantage. It is a power which you have developed slowly and patiently through many seemingly insurmountable dilemmas, and to lose sight of it now would be to set up a dangerous stumbling block in your life. Know that you are strong enough to make it through this stressful time without losing any of your self-esteem.

It is true that predicaments like the one you are now experiencing are a tremendous drain on the personal resources needed in life to achieve and maintain well-being. Your storehouse of potentials, however, is not a shallow pool. By taking inventory of your strongest qualities and looking at them honestly, you will be able to use what you see in your total self-image as the means by which to get back to the business of your life, your future. At this moment you are actually in the middle of the process of determining the outcome of the separation with which you are now confronted.

Work with the thoughts and beliefs that empower you. You are the only one who can filter out the useless forces from your own conception of yourself, forces such as guilt and self-blame. By concentrating on the best of the elements which make up your total image of yourself, you will be able to come through this experience complete and prepared for your own growth and development.

Self-Image

Describe the image you have of yourself without
the presence of the person from whom you are
now separating.

_____

_____

_____

_____

What incident in your relationship may have created in
you the feeling of worthlessness?

_____

_____

_____

_____

What are the ideals that guide your life?

_____

_____

_____

_____

What are the principles that guide your life?

_____

_____

_____

_____

What qualities about yourself do you want to keep?

_____

_____

_____

_____

What qualities about yourself do you want to change?

_____

_____

_____

_____

What new qualities do you want to add to your life?

_____

_____

_____

_____

Relax, and for 10 minutes reflect on the one word that best describes you. Record your thoughts and feelings.

_____

_____

_____

_____

_____

_____

_____

_____

_____

Responsibility

There is no duty we so much underrate
as the duty of being happy.

You are responsible for your world. At every major turn of events, you must be accountable for the way in which you are conducting your life. Now that you are in the process of facing the reality of separation from a loved one, you are choosing the direction which the rest of your life will take. And, of course, you hold yourself responsible for the choices you make in life.

Your decision to enter into a relationship was an indication of your confidence in life. This same confidence must be your guiding force now as you assess your present situation. You have to answer only to yourself, both for what has already taken place in your life and for what course you choose for meeting the terms of your future growth.

To look at the events of your life as some network of outside forces acting upon you is to lose sight of the primary role which you play in the development of your own destiny. Always be conscious of the responsibility you must assume for the way things develop around you. This consciousness is the cornerstone of a mature approach to reality.

Your ego is, in and of itself, a positive force. It represents an essential part of your instinct to protect yourself, thus allowing you to confront life's challenges effectively. However, like any positive force taken to extremes, an exaggeration of your ego can only lead you to defeat. Your responsibility to yourself should not be confused with an unbending impulse to protect your own belief system at all costs. The image which you have of yourself has been tested over and again by you. It is firmly in place. Clearly it is your responsibility to maintain the powers which are already yours and to use them for developing new ones. This must be done with a clear mind and in a spirit of humility.

Your own existence is only one life force in conjunction with the rest of humanity. Your actions have a direct effect not only on you but on everyone with whom you come into contact. Life is a process of interdependence. At every step in the formation of this new world which you are creating, you must look at your decisions and actions with an honest sense of perspective. By constantly holding yourself accountable for the way in which you personally mesh with the total fabric of life, you will assure yourself of the harmony which leads to growth.

Responsibility

"You create your own experiences either by causing them or allowing them to happen." What do you think about this statement?

_____

_____

_____

_____

_____

_____

For what occurrences in this past relationship do you not take responsibility?

_____

_____

_____

_____

_____

What blame are you placing on someone else for your separation?

_____

_____

_____

_____

_____

Were there times when you could have separated from the other person but instead made a conscious choice to stay in the relationship?

_____

_____

_____

_____

What is a positive ego?

_____

_____

_____

_____

What is a negative ego?

_____

_____

_____

_____

Relax, and for 10 minutes reflect on the strength derived from knowing you are responsible for the choices you make in life. Record your thoughts and feelings.

_____

_____

_____

_____

_____

_____

Acceptance

I accept the universe!

Margaret Fuller

Take hold of yourself and accept yourself for what you are now. Avoid the natural tendency toward trying to imagine the past as it could have been. Such thinking is a trap which can only immobilize you. What really happened is already clear to you. What could have been is nonexistent.

It is important that you develop now a willingness to see things as they really are. In order to accomplish this, it will be necessary to break down any barriers which may be blocking a clear perception of the present situation. These barriers were originally constructed by you, in an attempt to camouflage painful aspects of the separation. Know that in order to let go of your pain, you will have to acknowledge and accept its existence. And then you will need to accept two things: the way in which this situation relates to the person from whom you are separating and your interpretation of how this difficult situation affects you and the other person.

You can see that it is not possible, nor is it desirable, to try to change the other person. To attempt changing another is a frustrating and useless approach to the resolution of your dilemma. Show respect for the one whom you are leaving.

Accept the pain of your present experience and explore all the positive outcomes of this major change in both of your lives. Accept the fact that the other person is also in the process of moving toward the creation of a new and meaningful life. This acceptance will provide you with the space and energy you will need in going forward with your own life.

Come to terms with yourself and be willing to enter into the flow of moving toward the realization of your own potential. Self-acceptance is of the utmost importance at this time. You have found within yourself the capability of accepting the pain of the present reality. You are equally capable of appreciating the satisfaction which awaits you as you gain complete acceptance of yourself.

Acceptance

Describe the present reality of your separation.

_____

_____

_____

_____

_____

What was it about your separation that you found most
difficult to accept?

_____

_____

_____

_____

What steps can you take to overcome that difficulty?

_____

_____

_____

_____

What in your relationship would you have wanted
to change?

_____

_____

_____

_____

In what ways are you attempting to change the person from whom you are now separating?

_____

_____

_____

_____

What is the type of relationship you now want to have with the person from whom you are separating?

_____

_____

_____

_____

What strengths and powers of yours are you denying?

_____

_____

_____

_____

Relax, and for 10 minutes reflect on self-acceptance. Record your thoughts and feelings.

_____

_____

_____

_____

_____

_____

Feelings

The most important part of man's existence, that part where he most truly lives and is aware of living, lies entirely within the domain of personal feeling.

Joyce Cary

Your feelings represent the way in which you react to your perception of the world around you. As such, they are fundamental indicators of what you understand to be the truth. At this time, it is especially important that you see your situation as realistically as possible. You will first have to acknowledge your feelings in order to be able to free yourself from those negative feelings which are standing in your way.

Denial is usually the first response to a breakup. Pretending that the separation is not really happening, however, only delays the process of letting go to which you have committed yourself. Try to work through this feeling by not attempting to expect more than the reality of the situation in which you find yourself. Once you rid yourself of denial and accept the breakup of the relationship, you can truly begin the process of letting go.

Anxiety is also a natural reaction to the pain of separation. It is the feeling of uncertainty about the future and it can be real or imaginary. But your anxiety can be alleviated once you accept the fact that you are capable of overcoming the difficulties of a separation one step at a time. The fear of not being able to cope is resolved through an honest acceptance of the powers which you know are yours.

In letting go, let go of your anger as well and heal your emotional wounds. Expressing anger is a healthy response to a stressful situation, as long as it is expressed in an appropriate manner. But overreacting is as unhealthy as not reacting at all. Because you feel yourself to be hurt, the temptation may exist to hurt the other person. Rise above this feeling by being in total control of your situation. Express your anger with kindness, openness and honesty.

Unwarranted guilt is one of the most counterproductive of human feelings. If you have done something which you know was wrong, real guilt should lead you to seek forgiveness. During these initial stages of your separation, reexamine your belief system. Be kind to yourself and ask what is best for you. Realize that it is never possible to meet all the expectations another person has of you. There will always be the feeling that you could have done more. Transfer this feeling into the opposite of negative guilt: positive constructive action. You will be a better person. Do the same with any negative feelings which you encounter during this painful time. Confront them openly and with courage, transforming them into the positive energies which will lead you through all the difficulties of letting go.

Feelings

Describe your honest feelings about this separation which you are now experiencing.

_____

_____

_____

_____

_____

Which particular incident in the relationship made you feel most angry?

_____

_____

_____

_____

How did you really want to respond to that anger-producing situation?

_____

_____

_____

_____

Was there any incident in your relationship that caused you to feel shame?

_____

_____

_____

_____

Was there any incident in you relationship that caused you to feel guilt?

_____

_____

_____

_____

Was there any incident that made you feel resentment toward the person from whom you are separating?

_____

_____

_____

_____

On a separate sheet of paper, write a letter to the person from whom you are separating. Express in that letter all the anger, hurt, hatred, guilt, resentment and repressed feelings you may be experiencing. Tomorrow read the letter and add to it. The following day, read the letter once again and add to it. Then, in a safe manner, burn the letter.

Relax, and for 10 minutes reflect on the peacefulness of feeling emotional harmony. Record your thoughts and feelings.

_____

_____

_____

_____

_____

_____

Learning

All experience is an arch to build upon.

Henry Brooks Adams

See your present crisis for what it really is. You are not stuck in the middle of an incomprehensible situation. What is happening to you now is an integral part of the continuity of learning. The knowledge which you are gaining about yourself and others at this time will serve as the groundwork of your future decisions and actions. While some learning situations are joyous in nature, others are characterized by pain and suffering.

The anguish which you are feeling now represents a necessary stage in your progress. It is true that you must seek to overcome your pain as soon as possible. You realize, however, that you can only go beyond your present suffering by recognizing its existence and actually living through it. You have at your disposal already the sum of painful situations which you have come through successfully. Learning experiences build upon one another. You are now acquiring an even greater ability to cope with adversity. The learning process is a constant form of accomplishment.

Things happen for a reason and a purpose. The events of your life are not isolated fragments. Reflect on the connections between this phase of your experience and the other challenging periods which have strengthened you to this point. This particular step in your life represents the gaining of new information to be used in your evolution as an individual and as a successful participant in society. And you realize you are not alone in your experiences. The people with whom you will want to formulate new relationships in the near future will also have lived through similar conditions.

The open acceptance of all dimensions of learning leads to the discovery of truth. Each difficulty that you are now confronting represents a facet of your development of self-knowledge. You are getting to know yourself better by means of a separation from a loved one. Confront yourself. Look upon this phase of your life as one of the most valuable growth experiences ever presented to you. Learning and growth go hand in hand. You are truly in the process of coming to grips with yourself.

Your self-knowledge is the basis of your interaction with others. Look at yourself honestly at this time, recognizing your strengths as well as your weaknesses. The more realistic you are in your self-evaluation, the more prepared you will be for discovering your potential to share with others what you have learned in life.

Learning

Describe your most fundamental need prior to entering into the relationship with the person from whom you are now separating.

_____

_____

_____

_____

_____

Was that fundamental need satisfied?

_____

_____

_____

_____

What is your most fundamental need now?

_____

_____

_____

How will you satisfy that need?

_____

_____

_____

_____

What new learning have you derived from
your separation?

_____

_____

_____

_____

What quality most attracted you to the person from
whom you are now separating?

_____

_____

_____

_____

How can you incorporate or enhance that quality
in yourself?

_____

_____

_____

_____

Relax, and for 10 minutes reflect on what it would be
like to have total awareness. Record your thoughts
and feelings.

_____

_____

_____

_____

_____

Thoughts

Human thought is the process by which human ends are ultimately answered.

Daniel Webster

Your thoughts are one of the principal sources of your power to control your own destiny. There are some important aspects of the thought process with which you are probably already familiar. You may know that your thoughts are capable of altering bodily functions. In some instances, in the martial arts, for example, a change in thoughts can bring about a change in actual physical power. In a similar manner, the way in which you deal with your thoughts during this time of separation can determine the measure of success you will have in working through your conflict.

Think your thoughts out to the very end and you will see that your painful situation is not as extreme as you had perhaps believed. Realize that past situations in which you have found yourself cannot be changed; your perception of these experiences, however, is within your control. You have within you the capacity for changing any negative thoughts into positive ones.

By working with each negative thought individually, you will begin to understand your ability to master your own thought processes. Two thoughts cannot occupy the same space in consciousness. And it takes several seconds after a thought arises in the brain to identify the thought context to which it belongs, to decide to change it, and to make that change. Blocking or obstructing any negative thought, you understand, is only self-defeating. Even the most negative thoughts are ultimately subject to the form which you give to them. You will believe only what you choose to believe, what you tell yourself to believe.

Of course you are attempting, as much as possible, during this difficult period, not to dwell on thoughts about the other person. And you should be trying as well to give less attention to past negative thoughts. But you also realize that it is your responsibility to yourself to challenge any unpleasant thought when it rises up before you, so as to clear the way for a healthier thought process. After thinking a negative thought concerning your breakup and working through that thought, let it be clear to you that the outcome of that thought will be positive because of your will to make it so. Then make your next thought this: "I desire to let go." By doing so, you will confirm your original goal to deal with all the necessary stages of this painful time in your life. And you will be prepared to master and shape the thoughts which accompany you in this process of arriving at a positive outcome to your separation.

Thoughts

Describe the most painful thought you have about
your separation.

_____

_____

_____

_____

_____

Change that painful thought into a positive statement.

_____

_____

_____

_____

_____

Allow that painful thought to play out to its final
conclusion. What steps can you take to survive that final
conclusion?

_____

_____

_____

_____

_____

_____

What positive thoughts have guided you through difficult situations?

_____

_____

_____

_____

How do you change your negative thoughts?

_____

_____

_____

_____

_____

What new thoughts do you want to have to guide your future?

_____

_____

_____

_____

_____

Relax, and for 10 minutes reflect on what it would be like to have total conscious control of all your thoughts. Record your thoughts and feelings.

_____

_____

_____

_____

_____

Friends

A friend is a person with whom
I may be sincere.
Before him I may think aloud.

Ralph Waldo Emerson

The gift of friendship ranks among the greatest
blessings of this life. It is a force which consistently
proves its own validity and virtue through good times as
well as bad. Your friends are those who take joy in your
happiness, as you do in theirs. Similarly, you suffer
willingly for one another during times of distress. Just as
your friends are here now to stand beside you in your
difficulty, they are also very anxious to see you move on
through this period of stress. They wish to share with
you in the positive outcome which you are going to
make of this situation.

Consider some of the ways in which your friends can
help you through this difficult phase of your life. One of
the most useful means of working out your present
dilemma is the process of verbalization. Talk openly and
honestly with your friends about your present crisis, just
as you encourage them to do when life has presented
them with some obstacle. This will allow you to release
those pent-up frustrations which can only hold back your

liberation from the pain you are experiencing. Who can place a value on the feedback provided by conversations with a friend?

Select the friend or friends in whom you wish to confide at this time with intelligence and fairness. To choose someone who is a close friend both to you and to the person from whom you are separating could result in creating more stress for all three of you, since that friend would be forced to take sides. Your goal at this moment is to release yourself and others from as much suffering as possible; so it would be wise for you to place your trust now in a friend whose loyalty is dedicated to you.

You may feel that the nature of your crisis is such that even your best friends cannot succeed in helping you to unravel completely the knot of emotions you are now living through. Seeking professional assistance for your problems can be an indication of a realistic understanding of the complex nature of your difficulties. In no way does it represent a betrayal of friendship on your part. In fact, if you choose this course of action, you can discuss it freely with close friends.

Your true friends will gladly bear with you, no matter what path you choose for arriving at the positive outcome toward which you are now headed. And when you arrive there, your joy will be theirs as well.

Friends

Make a list of friends who can help you through
your separation.

_____

_____

_____

_____

Are there any obstacles that prevent you from asking
someone for help?

_____

_____

_____

_____

With what friend or counselor would you now want to
discuss your separation?

_____

_____

_____

_____

What are the expectations you have of your friend
or counselor?

_____

_____

_____

_____

_____

What various aspects of your separation would you be willing to discuss with your friend or counselor?

_____

_____

_____

_____

In what specific aspect of your separation can your friend or counselor help you most?

_____

_____

_____

_____

What organizations can help you through your separation?

_____

_____

_____

_____

_____

Relax, and for 10 minutes reflect on the value of friendship. Record your thoughts and feelings.

_____

_____

_____

_____

_____

Activity

Whether you'll try for the goal that's afar
Or be contented to stay just where you are.
Take it or leave. Here's something to do,
Just think it over. It's all up to you!

Elizabeth Barrett Browning

The severe stress of a separation tends to immobilize the people involved and it is for this reason that your ability to spring back to action is of the utmost significance at this time. Meet your present crisis with a sense of vigor and liveliness. These are the perfect antidotes to the sluggishness that comes with depression and confusion. The sooner you begin to engage in positive and constructive action, the sooner you will feel the healing process moving within you.

Mental and physical activities are of equal importance in restoring yourself to a healthy and productive state. The mind and body work as a unit in the achievement of the vitality necessary for overcoming inertia. Return quickly to the activities in both of these realms that give you pleasure and increase your feelings of strength and purpose. By immersing yourself in the things which intensify your awareness of the forward thrust of life, you will place yourself back on the path of the productive future which lies ahead of you.

Challenge yourself as well to become involved in an activity which you have never before attempted. Set this new horizon for yourself now, by taking the first steps in accomplishing a goal which you had perhaps thought about in the past, without ever actually confronting it face to face. Approach this activity with total self-confidence. Bend with the new experience, accepting all its facets, its possibilities. Move into this adventure with passion and trust.

Take up an activity which will put you at risk. What will you learn or accomplish without risk? You know that taking a chance at something is the only real way of truly coming to grips with it. Love itself takes risks as part of its natural course. Engage yourself in a risk-taking situation with confidence in your heart. Grow from the experience, moving forward at all times from where you are now. Make your trust in life active.

Embrace openly another of life's most rewarding actions, that of extending yourself to someone else, doing good for someone else. The energies which flow between you and the person to whom you reach out are as beneficial to you as they are to the other person. Your life is ultimately the total of your actions and, more importantly, of your interactions with others. Giving of yourself places you into active participation in life. Sharing with others strengthens your own character, keeping you firmly grounded in your path toward progress.

Activity

What activities would most facilitate your physical well-being?

_____

_____

_____

_____

What activities would most facilitate your emotional growth?

_____

_____

_____

_____

What activities would most facilitate your intellectual growth?

_____

_____

_____

_____

What activities would most facilitate your spiritual growth?

_____

_____

_____

_____

What action can you take today that would be beneficial for someone else?

_____

_____

_____

_____

What activity can you begin that would bring you the most joy?

_____

_____

_____

_____

What activity can you begin that would bring the most love into your life?

_____

_____

_____

_____

Relax, and for 10 minutes feel the natural energy that is a part of you. Record your thoughts and feelings.

_____

_____

_____

_____

_____

_____

_____

Change of Scenery

The soul of a journey is liberty,
perfect liberty, to think, feel,
do just as one pleases.
We go on a journey chiefly
to be free of all impediments
and of all inconveniences;
to leave ourselves behind.

William Hazlitt

Much of the negative energy involved in a separation from a loved one comes to be associated with the physical locales in which the relationship to that person grew and then disintegrated. This is a feeling which is all too familiar to anyone who is experiencing the pain of separation. It is natural for you to identify certain places with the emotions connected to experiences you have lived through in those places. And it is just as natural for you to wish to remove yourself from those surroundings, so as to be distanced from settings which now seem to work against you as you attempt to remake your life. Take the opportunity to give yourself a change of scenery, since the effect of such a change is one of refreshment and inspiration.

As soon as possible you might begin to take small trips, perhaps away from the town or city in which you live. Traveling with a friend can be an excellent way of removing yourself from troublesome contexts and of engaging in the undisturbed company of someone with whom you enjoy spending time. Or you may choose to travel on your own. Such an experience has the benefit of placing you in a situation where you can reach out to new acquaintances or take advantage of peaceful solitary meditation in a setting which is free from all associations.

These small journeys away from your immediate context are beneficial as a needed temporary relief from a stressful situation. Most importantly, however, you know that you are in the process of developing a new outlook with which to readjust to the setting in which you live permanently. The ultimate value of what you experience during your travels will have to be incorporated into your life, once you have returned to your familiar setting. The true benefit derived from travel has to do with the development of your ability for discovery. In your journeys you are constantly surrounded with a sense of newness and vitality. Learn to appreciate the excitement associated with discovery, and look upon this stimulation as an ongoing experience. Carry this excitement home with you.

Enjoy the place in which you find yourself. It is within your potential to reinterpret the reality in which you live. You are now challenging yourself to discover the new and positive dimensions of the setting in which you are restructuring your life.

Change of Scenery

Change the route you normally take to and from work or to wherever you go. What new route would that be?

_____

_____

_____

_____

After using the new route, list the discoveries you made.

_____

_____

_____

_____

What place gives you the greatest sense of serenity?

_____

_____

_____

_____

Where would it be most helpful for you to travel at this time?

_____

_____

_____

_____

What places allow you to reflect on the beauty of nature?

_____

_____

_____

_____

_____

What places allow you to have the most fun?

_____

_____

_____

_____

What places bring you the most joy?

_____

_____

_____

_____

Relax, and for 10 minutes reflect on an imaginary place
that would be peaceful for you. Record your thoughts
and feelings.

_____

_____

_____

_____

_____

_____

Laughter

We are all here for a spell;
get all the good laughs you can.

Will Rogers

The joy of living is as much within your grasp now as it ever was. Remember this and reach out at this time toward the delightful things which life has to offer. The transition in which you now find yourself is a movement toward the discovery of the joy of new beginnings. Assert your right to take pleasure in the people and situations which bring you happiness. Look at the light side of your circumstances. Have the courage to laugh.

Life has shown you countless times the immeasurable value of laughter. You know that once you are able to talk about an unfortunate experience, it is under your control; and once you can laugh at it, you have conquered it. Even your most serious past mistakes contain some aspect of humor. Recognize that this is true. When you succeed in laughing at yourself for your own misfortunes, you put into motion a new set of thought patterns and open yourself once again to the recognition of your potential for happiness. Thus, it is within your power to lift the cloud of negativity which causes one to forget that life is to be enjoyed.

Even on the physical level, laughter is known to calm and soothe the body and to relieve it from pain. In a similar way, it brightens the entire spirit and awakens it to an awareness of the beauty of life. Why continue to dwell in the world of bitterness, when laughter opens the door to delight? Just as you have lived many happy and humorous experiences in past relationships, it is now time to create new situations in which you can be brought back into contact with the cheerfulness of life. Such contact should be a daily occurrence. It is only when we see the comical side of so many of our daily experiences and treat them in a lighthearted manner that we can relax to the point of being comfortable with ourselves and with those around us.

Just as you have faced your pain and confusion openly during this separation, you should live up to your capacity for being joyful as well. Open yourself to the humorous dimension of life. It surrounds you and invites you at every turn. Share your amusement and your willingness to laugh with others and the joy you impart to them will return to you and strengthen you.

Laughter

What can you do to have more fun in your life?

_____

_____

_____

_____

What entertainers can you see who would make
you laugh?

_____

_____

_____

_____

What humorous movies or videos would you like to see?

_____

_____

_____

_____

What humorous T.V. shows would you like to see?

_____

_____

_____

_____

What humorous books would you like to read?

_____

_____

_____

_____

_____

Which of your friends make you laugh?

_____

_____

_____

_____

_____

Describe the funniest experience you have ever had.

_____

_____

_____

_____

_____

Relax, and for 10 minutes feel totally happy. Record
your thoughts and feelings.

_____

_____

_____

_____

_____

_____

The Future

I shall walk eager still for what Life holds
Although it seems the hard road will not end
One never knows the beauty round the bend!

Anna Blake Mezquida

With every form of adversity comes the seed of an equal or greater benefit. Look upon your future as the bright outcome of the storm you are living through during this time of your separation. Most importantly, you must believe in the positive value of this outcome, which will perhaps require a change in your perspective. If you keep in mind the idea that all things happen for a reason and a purpose, it will be easier for you to create out of your future a positive result of your painful experience.

The future will be happier. Make this your guiding principle. Meditate upon it; listen to the bright messages of things to come. Understand that if you have been capable of getting through the chaos of this separation, you are that much more prepared to be the master of what lies ahead of you. Think in these terms. Give yourself credit for the courage with which you are meeting your present circumstances and accept the fact that this very positive quality of yours is the springboard toward a positive future.

The future is the greatest source of inspiration that you have. It represents an entire world of possibilities. These possibilities are clearly within your reach only if you will develop now the proper attitude toward your own future potentials. Make an attempt to imagine and visualize this future. Set goals for yourself which are stepping stones in the direction of that bright future as you imagine it. Before you now lies the greatest opportunity of all: the chance to realize your own growth and development to its maximum. Think of the experience of your separation as the first stage in the movement toward a better future life for yourself and for those whom you will encounter as you weave the texture of things as they are to be. You are now one step higher in the understanding of human relationships. And that understanding, without a doubt, is the most significant of all in the creation of a meaningful and successful future.

The optimism which is necessary in order to make things happen in your favor lies entirely within your grasp. Your whole future depends upon the attitude with which you approach it. Make that attitude the most positive one imaginable. Remember that your future is everything and that you have the power to make it as bright as you wish.

The Future

What are your dreams for the future?

_____

_____

_____

_____

_____

_____

What are your desires for the future?

_____

_____

_____

_____

_____

What may be preventing you from having the kind of future you most want?

_____

_____

_____

_____

_____

What choices do you want to make now for your future?

_____

_____

_____

_____

_____

In what areas of your life do you want to have
more abundance?

_____

_____

_____

_____

_____

What do you want the future "you" to be like?

_____

_____

_____

_____

Relax, and for 10 minutes reflect on having a happy
future. Record your thoughts and feelings.

_____

_____

_____

_____

Communication

Self-expression must pass into
communication for its fulfillment.

Helen Hull

The process of letting go is naturally one of deep introspection, of looking into yourself in order to understand yourself better. This self-examination, however, should be understood as a preliminary step toward the act of conveying to others, in the clearest manner possible, your thoughts and feelings concerning your present state and your plans for the future. Take advantage of your ability to see your own situation realistically; use this ability as a means of preparing yourself for as open a dialogue as possible with the other person. As you gain knowledge and strength in your determination to let go, you gain the means for communicating to your former partner your intention to do so and the steps you plan to take in doing it.

If the channels of communication between you and the other person are already open, you may want to discuss together some of the contents of this book and what it is you are learning from it. This could enable both of you to have a clearer understanding of each other's position in this difficult situation and could serve as a bridge between you for the interchange of ideas and feelings.

If such is not the case, then you should seek to find the most sincere means of communication possible for the expression of your thoughts to the other person. This may take the form of a personal visit; or you may have to achieve this important step by means of a telephone call or a letter.

Whatever manner you find best for reaching out to the other person, always keep in mind the necessity for doing so. Communication removes the uncertainty which all too often clouds the reality of a separation. It is this uncertainty which prolongs a painful situation and prevents those who are separating from coming to grips with the decisions which will be necessary for meeting the serious challenges presented by separation.

Communication helps you to become more committed to your original goal of wanting to let go. Once you have conveyed openly and honestly to the other person what your intentions are, your energies will be directed outward and you will begin to feel a sense of freedom from built-up negative emotions. Your goal is to move forward, and in order to do this you will have to place yourself in a position of being able to communicate with the rest of the world. Your communication with the person from whom you are separating is an invaluable step in this direction.

Communication

In what ways are you not being honest with yourself concerning the nature of your breakup?

_____

_____

_____

_____

In what ways are you not being honest with the person from whom you are separating?

_____

_____

_____

_____

What is it that you want to directly communicate to the person from whom you are separating?

_____

_____

_____

_____

"The final response to the ending of a relationship should be one of gratitude." What do you think about that statement?

_____

_____

_____

_____

What is it that you are grateful for in this
past relationship?

_____

_____

_____

_____

_____

What may be preventing you from expressing your
gratitude to the person from whom you are separating?

_____

_____

_____

_____

Relax, and for 10 minutes feel the satisfaction you
receive when you respond to your emotions honestly.
Record your thoughts and feelings.

_____

_____

_____

_____

_____

_____

Music

Music is the universal language of mankind.

Henry Wadsworth Longfellow

One of the purest forms for the expression of ideas and emotions is music. This is a gift which is always at your disposal. During this time of separation, it can serve as a means of relaxation and inspiration. By choosing wisely the kind of music with which you surround yourself, you can in many ways prepare for the challenges which await you in this transformation you are undergoing.

Choose music to listen to which will create for you an oasis of peace in which you can meditate on the rhythms of life and thus strengthen yourself. The harp and the flute, for example, are instruments whose music is conducive to such a state of relaxation. Meditative music helps us to suspend our worries and to replenish the peaceful energies which are necessary for emotional balance. In this period you owe it to yourself to achieve such a balance, so that you will be able to confront your future with a sense of calm reassurance.

In addition to listening to live or recorded music which will provide for you a healthy frame of mind, you have within you a wealth of personal musical experiences. From your memory you can draw on many forms of music which bring about in you a positive effect. You can bring to life within yourself melodies which remove you from your feelings of solitude or produce in you good feelings about yourself and about the world in which you live. Enjoy these personal musical delights by singing or humming them to yourself. By doing so, you will appreciate more thoroughly the continuity which music has had in your life and you will allow yourself to reap more abundantly its benefits.

One of music's most important dimensions is the communication that it creates among people. Music brings people together. Go to the places where music puts you in happy contact with others. In the public sphere, dance is the counterpart to music. Dance turns the spiritual quality of music into the physical. Dance to the music.

Allow music to work its full powers upon you at this time. Take advantage of its potential for healing wounds and creating a bridge for interpersonal communication. What you are truly seeking now is harmony within yourself and between you and the rest of the world. Music is one of the most beautiful expressions of this harmony.

Music

If you were to write your own song to guide you through the letting-go process, what would be the title of that song?

_____

_____

What would be the first verse of that song?

_____

_____

_____

_____

_____

What would be the chorus of that song?

_____

_____

_____

_____

What songs do you find most inspiring?

_____

_____

_____

_____

What instrumentals do you find most peaceful?

_____

_____

_____

_____

What songs have messages that are not helpful in the letting-go process?

_____

_____

_____

_____

What one song would you sing or hum to yourself to uplift you in a moment of sadness?

_____

_____

Relax, and for 10 minutes reflect on a particular sound of nature. Record your thoughts and feelings.

_____

_____

_____

_____

_____

_____

_____

_____

_____

Autosuggestion

Every day, in every way,
I am getting better and better.

Your imagination is certainly among the most profound of your personal resources. The ability to create images, to visualize, is what enables you to link together the subconscious and conscious dimensions of your thoughts. That which you choose to visualize or imagine as your reality will condition, to a great degree, the way in which your reality will actually occur. So much of the real outcome of this separation you are experiencing will depend upon the way in which you envision that outcome. The power to shape reality is yours; and it begins with your power to visualize your life as you know it ought to be.

The suggestions you make to yourself, by means of what you visualize on the subconscious level, are the building blocks for your real behavior. This is because the human mind is constantly forming new connections between subconscious and conscious life. Ask yourself: What is my image of the positive resolution of my situation? How would I feel if this resolution had actually been realized? What would my day be like today?

Get into the habit of visualizing the details of your new life as you see them in your mind's eye. Be constantly aware that the two levels of reality, the subconscious and the conscious, flow easily into one another. This awareness is what will enable you to transform your thoughts into actions.

Once you have accepted the intimate connection between what is suggested by the mind and what is actually done, begin immediately to act as though the resolution of your difficulties had already occurred. There are virtually no limits to what can be accomplished when you begin to live out the images which you have created for yourself. Past habits which impeded your total development can be broken. New and positive behavior can be visualized and lived out. Within a matter of days you can bring to reality the first stage of your liberation from suffering as you visualize it. In a few weeks you will be well on your way to living out completely the reality you have suggested to yourself.

The recognition of your desire to let go is something you have already accomplished. Now your expectations and the genuine belief that you can achieve the goal of letting go will clarify your vision of the successful realization of that goal. This vision, in turn, must come to fruition by means of your ability to act it out in real life. It is your vision of your positive reality. Begin to live it.

Autosuggestion

What are your thoughts concerning the
unconscious mind?

_____

_____

_____

_____

_____

What are your thoughts concerning the
subconscious mind?

_____

_____

_____

_____

_____

What are your thoughts concerning the conscious mind?

_____

_____

_____

_____

What are your thoughts concerning visualization as a
means to enhance your life?

_____

_____

_____

_____

What steps can you take to increase peace and harmony within yourself?

_____

_____

_____

_____

What steps can you take to increase the power of your imagination?

_____

_____

_____

_____

What positive affirmations would best help you to let go completely?

_____

_____

_____

_____

Relax, and for 10 minutes reflect on the intelligence that is alive in every cell of your body. Record your thoughts and feelings.

_____

_____

_____

_____

_____

Strength

The turning point in the process of growing
up is when you discover the core of strength
within you that survives all hurt.

Max Lerner

Now that you have made the decision to let go, be
constantly aware that you have within you the
strength to carry out that decision in such a way that
what lies ahead of you can only lead to success.
Remember that it was your own fortitude which allowed
you to face honestly the need for this separation. And
your own inner resources provided you with the capacity
for going through with the only course of action which
could lead you to a meaningful direction for your life.
You are now embarking on a time in your life when you
will need to make other very difficult decisions. Be
convinced that the same inner strength which has
brought you this far will continue to enable you to take
charge of your life.

It is natural for you to seek the help of loved ones and
friends during this trying period. Such help, when
offered, should be accepted and utilized by you with a
sense of appreciation and love. Keep in mind, however,
that the burden ultimately lies on your own shoulders

and that you are indeed strong enough to bear this weight with a positive attitude; and that, if necessary, you can stand alone in doing it. Your task is to heal your wounds now so that you will be prepared to contribute to your own growth and development and, in turn, to that of others.

Continue to reevaluate your decisions as you work through each phase of this breakup. At each step, have the courage to do what is best for you. Be strong-minded and resilient in your efforts to let go. Every decision you make during this time should reflect your awareness of your own power to succeed. Let no one intimidate you. With perseverance you will see your way through all the decisions necessary for getting you back to your normal self.

By drawing upon the power which you have worked so hard at developing, you will be able to meet any eventuality caused by this separation. Be steadfast in your determination to avoid playing the role of victim or martyr. Think of the worst possible scenario in connection with this breakup. Is it that bad? Surely not. The most difficult scenario, that of the process of deciding to let go, is one which you have already mastered because of your inner strength. That same strength is still yours for meeting every challenge that stands before you. Continue to be firm in your decision. Walk forward courageously.

Strength

What is the greatest strength a person can possess?

_____

_____

How can you enhance that strength in yourself?

_____

_____

_____

_____

What are some of your strengths?

_____

_____

_____

_____

What new strengths do you want to add to your life?

_____

_____

_____

_____

In what instances have you allowed yourself to be
dominated or manipulated by others?

_____

_____

_____

_____

What does self-pity mean for you?

_____

_____

_____

_____

_____

In what ways can you increase your self-confidence
in order to cope with any challenge presented by
this separation?

_____

_____

_____

_____

_____

Relax, and for 10 minutes reflect on your greatest
strength. Record your thoughts and feelings.

_____

_____

_____

_____

_____

_____

_____

_____

Giving

When I give I give myself.

Walt Whitman

At this time, it is natural for you to be thinking about all that you have given to that person from whom you are now separating. Not only is this natural; it is necessary, in order for you to establish a better understanding of your potential for future growth. To dwell upon the idea that you gave too much or too little, however, is counterproductive and will keep you tied to the past. You must be able to see the act of giving as being intimately connected to that which you receive in your life experiences.

In order to have a clearer knowledge of the relationship between giving and receiving, you will have to consider what your motivation was in giving something in the first place. Where you feel pain or resentment for what you have given, the guiding force behind the giving was itself negative. It was based upon a calculation of what you expected to receive in return. The benefits of love cannot be calculated. Where you feel genuine joy for having given, it is because your giving was really a sharing of yourself. Giving as sharing of oneself is the very foundation of love.

Your mind should be focused on the spiritual sharing which was the core of your relationship. This is not to say that the material concerns involved in this separation are not important. They are; but they are secondary to your development as a person capable of sharing a life with someone else. And you should treat them as such. If there must be a division of shared material possessions, then go about making this division with a sense of fairness and love.

When you give freely, you are always the recipient. Keep this idea foremost in your mind. As you examine your past, try to recognize the occasions when your open sharing of yourself was the source of your joy and of your sense of freedom. Concentrate upon the experiences in which the love you received was the pure counterpart of the love you gave.

This period of separation affords you the opportunity to learn more about yourself and your potential for giving. Carry the fruits of the experiences you shared in the relationship into your present life. Practice freely the act of giving and of seeing this giving as a sharing of yourself. Life itself is the greatest giver of all. By realizing this, you will be at peace with yourself and capable of giving back to life your greatest gift—yourself.

Giving

Describe what unconditional giving means for you.

_____

_____

_____

_____

What qualities characterize a person who gives
unconditionally?

_____

_____

_____

What was your motivation for giving in
your relationship?

_____

_____

_____

What aspects of yourself did you want to give in
this relationship?

_____

_____

_____

_____

91

What further aspects of yourself do you want to give in the next relationship?

_____

_____

_____

_____

In what ways do you feel you have given more love than you received?

_____

_____

_____

_____

_____

What are some ways in which you can pamper yourself?

_____

_____

_____

_____

Relax, and for 10 minutes reflect on an unconditional gift of nature. Record your thoughts and feelings.

_____

_____

_____

_____

_____

Viewpoint

Each man sees what he carries in his heart.

Johann Wolfgang von Goethe

The way in which you view your present situation in its relation to the rest of your life is all important. Look upon this period of your experience as an opportunity for growth. Every moment of your life, in fact, represents such an opportunity, as long as you are willing to see it as such.

What separates success from failure is the way in which we perceive the possibilities inherent in all of life's circumstances. Even in your sorrow you can find joy if your viewpoint in reference to that sorrow allows you to do so. Your joy will consist of the understanding that sorrow has served to strengthen you for the future which you have already begun to live out.

The root of continued pain lies frequently in an error of perception. It lies in the refusal to see the positive aspects of every human act. A healthy outlook on even the most negative experience eliminates frustration and opens the way toward the kind of self-image which can direct any chain of events to a successful conclusion. How often have you worried about things that never came to pass? This was wasted energy; for even when what seemed insurmountable did come your way, you were more than prepared to live through your difficulties with a sense of accomplishment and strength. Your present situation is a perfect example of this ability of yours.

Shifting your perspective does not imply a dilution of your value system. On the contrary, changes in point of view from one of life's encounters to the next serve as a way of reinforcing the total structure of the accumulated values which guide your actions every day. Maintain that high level of esteem in which you originally held this relationship which is now ending. It was the circumstances alone which prevented its continued development.

Love itself is still at the top of your hierarchy of values. And this love can be understood in new ways, if you will permit yourself to look upon the nature of love in its myriad of forms. These include the desire to help make life better for your fellow human beings and the commitment to pursuing spiritual power and knowledge, especially self-knowledge.

You cannot change the events of your past. What you can change is the way in which you view the significance of these events and the place they occupy in the total mosaic of your existence. See them for what they really are, and build around them in such a way that the complete picture of this phase of your experience is in keeping with your ultimate vision of life.

Viewpoint

How do you perceive the separation which you are experiencing?

_____

_____

_____

_____

In what areas of your life have you grown as a result of your relationship with the person from whom you are now separating?

_____

_____

_____

_____

In what areas of your life do you want to continue growing?

_____

_____

_____

_____

How can you accelerate your growth?

_____

_____

_____

_____

What significant awareness have you gained from your relationship that will be of value to you?

_____

_____

_____

_____

_____

What can you do to put that awareness into action?

_____

_____

_____

_____

How can you continuously live that awareness?

_____

_____

_____

_____

Relax and for 10 minutes reflect on a positive outcome of your separation?

_____

_____

_____

_____

_____

Thinking

Reading furnishes our mind with
materials of knowledge; it is thinking
that makes what we read ours.

John Locke

In the process of thinking we are as much involved in
generating new choices for ourselves as we are in
gathering information based on past experiences. The
recognition of this power is what permits us to enlarge
our vision of the world and of our place within it. And
we can change our understanding of the world by changing the way we think.

During this period of transition it is important for
you to see that good thinking is controlled thinking.
Simply shifting from one emotion to another can only
bring confusion. Think first, sort out your thoughts;
and then give close attention to each of your emotions
in order to determine which are appropriate and which
are not. In this way, you control your emotions; they do
not control you.

All of us have many beliefs and attitudes which we
ourselves have already developed or which we have
simply accepted as being absolute. Some of these fundamental beliefs are essential, in order for us to maintain a

healthy sense of equilibrium within society. It should be clear, however, that some of our self-made or unquestioned notions may be blocking us from realizing the possibilities inherent in our lives. We are sometimes afraid to question the validity of new ways of looking at ourselves. Free your mind of these fears and be sensitive to everything around you. Start with no preconceived ideas and explore all the alternatives available to you. Only when you suspend judgment can you embark on the process of creative thinking.

So many new aspects of life will become apparent once you are willing to expand your capacity to think creatively. Investigate what you discover about yourself and your relationships, past and present. Take the knowledge which comes from this increased awareness of your reality and make it work to your advantage. You are the best judge of your present situation.

At this time you are in search of the truth about yourself. Uncovering this truth will involve the courage on your part to look at your separation realistically and to apply your thinking skills toward the resolution of your dilemma. This goal is clearly within your reach. Your willingness to examine every aspect of the alternatives before you is what will lead you in new directions.

By placing the meaning of your experiences in proper perspective you can go on to empower yourself. This will be accomplished by observing carefully the way in which you think.

Thinking

How can you further develop your ability to analyze situations?

_____

_____

_____

_____

What security did you once have in your relationship that you feel you have lost?

_____

_____

_____

_____

What are your alternatives for regaining that security?

_____

_____

_____

_____

In what ways can you show additional caring for someone who is important to you?

_____

_____

_____

_____

In what ways are all human beings equal?

_____

_____

_____

_____

Describe your ultimate journey in life.

_____

_____

_____

_____

How can you further develop your creative powers?

_____

_____

_____

_____

Relax, and for 10 minutes quiet your mind. Record your thoughts and feelings.

_____

_____

_____

_____

_____

_____

Fear

When I can read my title clear
to mansions in the skies,
I bid farewell to every fear,
and wipe my weeping eyes.

Isaac Watts

In this period of change you are living through you owe it to yourself to remove from your path all obstacles which might prevent you from realizing the new goals you have set for yourself. Fear is one of the greatest impediments to self-realization. And the fear of loneliness is one of the first emotions to be conquered during a time of separation, since it gives birth to a multitude of other fears which can only hinder your progress. You need to understand the nature of fear in order to overcome it. The anxiety you are feeling is rooted in a set of beliefs which are faulty.

One of these mistaken beliefs is that you are incapable of being alone, even for a limited period of time, and that to do so will render you helpless. While it is true that you must confront and understand your fears on your own in order to do away with them, this should not be equated with loneliness. Think of this period as one in which you are allowing yourself the freedom to come to terms with your own reality. This is the time when you must discover your erroneous beliefs and change them, so that they will no longer stand in your way. It is only by converting this fear into something positive that you can truly prevent the separation that fear creates between you and your own true feelings, thoughts and identity.

Fear also feeds upon another illogical belief at a time such as this: the belief that you do not love well enough. Simply stop for a moment and think of the qualities you possess for creating and maintaining meaningful inter-personal relationships and you will see that this fear, like so many, is imaginary. Think of the risks you run if you allow unrealistic fears to block your determination to see your way through this separation with a sense of self-love and a vision of the achievements which lie ahead of you.

Confront those fears which do have true substance. Look at them honestly and determine the course of action within your power for resolving them. These fears should be thought of as a challenge which you are more than prepared to meet.

The overwhelming majority of your preoccupations, however, have no real substance at all. They are the result of faulty beliefs. They are fears which have grown out of your unwillingness to accept your own strength and personal worth. Release yourself from them. Focus on your present reality. Love yourself. Place yourself in harmony with the core of your own spiritual strength and with your capacity to enrich your own life and the lives of others. In order to discover what is true, what is your destiny, you must demand freedom from all fears.

Fear

What was your greatest fear prior to entering into the relationship with the person from whom you are now separating?

_____

_____

_____

_____

Describe the greatest fear you have now.

_____

_____

_____

_____

Explain the origin of your fear you have now.

_____

_____

_____

_____

Describe the fear of loneliness.

_____

_____

_____

_____

What would be some of the beliefs of someone who fears loneliness?

_____

_____

_____

_____

How does one end loneliness?

_____

_____

_____

_____

What fears serve as positive boundaries that you would want to maintain?

_____

_____

_____

_____

Relax, and for 10 minutes feel loneliness. Record your thoughts and feelings.

_____

_____

_____

_____

_____

_____

_____

Moment to Moment

Hold every moment sacred.
Give each clarity and meaning,
each the weight of thine awareness,
each its true and due fulfillment.

Thomas Mann

Given the pain which you are now going through because of your separation from a loved one, there is a temptation to allow the mind to wander back into the negativity of recent past experiences. Overcome the temptation by insisting on centering yourself in the present. Seize the moment. If you allow this precious moment to slip by without appreciating it as part of the continuity of your life, then it will simply be added to the past, without ever having been truly lived. And it will be futile for you to attempt to take hold of it tomorrow. Now is the time to shape and develop this moment in a meaningful way. Only the present exists. And it belongs to you.

Immerse yourself totally in whatever your present activity involves. Keep your active participation in current projects foremost in your mind. Appreciate the value of what you are doing. The ultimate merit of your present endeavors lies in your ability to be the master of your thoughts and actions.

Every small step leads you to the achievement of great distances. Allow each step in your journey to be recognized for the immediate value which it represents. The more you are able to accept every moment of your existence, the more beautiful will be the outcome of the journey of all your moments as they become days, months and years. Self-awareness is not something which you are planning; it is a force which you are living from moment to moment. And your relationship to the rest of the world is grounded in your present frame of mind. The awareness you will need in order to move ahead is being formulated and reinforced at this very instant.

This is the moment which truly counts. Accept yourself in this moment for everything positive which you represent. And make this attitude a way of life. Your strength is drawn from the past and from your plans for the future. This strength can be validated, however, only in the present. Its continuity depends upon your decision to recognize that this is true.

You live in the here and now. Look around you and absorb what you see, understanding that the reality which surrounds you now is your essential field of action. It is true that your past is incorporated into the way in which you see your present. And the future gives you inspiration for what you are now doing. The fact remains, however, that this very moment represents the totality of your accumulated experiences and your future aspirations.

Moment to Moment

What can you do to stay focused in the present?

_____

_____

_____

_____

What meaningful action do you want to take today that will significantly help you to let go?

_____

_____

_____

_____

Describe what your day would be like if you had total security.

_____

_____

_____

_____

Describe what your day would be like if you loved yourself totally.

_____

_____

_____

_____

Describe what your day would be like if you had total understanding of your separation.

_____

_____

_____

_____

Describe what your day would be like if you were in harmony with everyone.

_____

_____

_____

_____

Describe what your day would be like if you were to let go completely.

_____

_____

_____

_____

Relax, and for 10 minutes focus on your heart. Record your thoughts and feelings.

_____

_____

_____

_____

Freedom

What other liberty is there worth having,
if we have not freedom and peace
in our minds?

H. D. Thoreau

One of the fundamental necessities for growth is freedom. Give yourself and the person from whom you are now separating permission to be free. It is clear that in the development of any healthy human relationship the mutual giving of freedom is essential. This period of separation which you are experiencing is an extension of the relationship itself. Freedom is just as important in this phase of separation as it was at any other stage in your association. By choosing freedom for yourself and the other person, you allow the door to be opened to a world of possibilities awaiting both of you. It would be unreasonable to prevent this opening in any way. Why deny yourself or others this opportunity?

To continue to dwell upon the bonds and restrictions which once may have defined, in part, your relationship would be to force yourself to remain in the field of negativity. Now it is important to see that what the two of you really owe to one another is a willingness to allow the other person to pursue life's challenges according to his or her own vision. You understand that everyone has the right to follow an individual plan for discovery and development, a plan unhampered by outside resistance. Take it upon yourself to put this understanding into action.

Begin to live as a free person, allowing the other person to do the same. Ultimately, you are bound to yourself and to a greater Power which unifies all the aspirations of mankind. When all of your commitments in life are seen in this light, freedom comes more easily.

The giving and taking of freedom is certainly one of the most difficult challenges with which you will be faced during this time of separation. It is natural to want to cling to what we already understand or think we understand. This clinging may give you a sense of security. But it is a false sense of security, one which can only prevent you and the other person from getting on with the business of the rest of life. Letting go demands freedom.

What lies ahead of you is nothing less than the infinite possibility of choices. As you look toward your future, you see before you ways which can lead you to your own greater development. Feel free to follow them.

Freedom

How will you know when you have completely let go?

_____

_____

_____

Describe what personal freedom means for you.

_____

_____

_____

_____

What aspects of your personality or circumstances
may be holding you back from experiencing
personal freedom?

_____

_____

_____

_____

In what ways may you be blocking the freedom of the
person from whom you are separating?

_____

_____

_____

What is the greatest freedom you can have?

_____

_____

_____

_____

Why do you want freedom?

_____

_____

_____

_____

How would your life change if you were completely free?

_____

_____

_____

_____

Relax, and for 10 minutes reflect on having fulfillment
in life. Record your thoughts and feelings.

_____

_____

_____

_____

_____

_____

_____

_____

A Dynamic Meditation

By completing the first section of this book you have demonstrated your strong commitment to transcend your suffering and to take your first steps on the path to fulfillment in life. You may choose to continue your journey with a dynamic meditation.

A dynamic meditation is standard meditation made more purposeful and powerful by visualization. Bringing forth a mental picture while you relax is like controlled daydreaming, but as you will discover, your results are determined in large part by what you picture.

Begin by reading several times the following guide to the meditation in order to acquaint yourself thoroughly with its contents. Allow your own imagination to lead you through those areas you may not fully understand.

After you have become thoroughly familiar with the contents of the meditation, you can make a cassette recording of the text using your own voice. This allows you to guide yourself through the meditation. Or you may want to have a close friend or acquaintance make the recording for you.

This is your personal meditation and you can make the recording as eloquent or as simple as you like.

Your Key To Letting Go
Relaxation

This meditation is intended to help you discover for yourself your own personal key to the essence of letting go.

Find a comfortable position, either lying down or sitting up.

Let your eyelids begin to relax. Gently close your eyes.

Let your breathing become calm. Let it become smooth and quiet.

What a wonderful feeling to allow yourself to relax! Surround yourself with silence and peace. Let your body and mind become still.

You are in total control of this guided visualization. You can accept or reject anything that is being said. You are always in total control.

Take a deep breath and, as you exhale, begin to relax your body. Start at the bottom of your body, telling each part of your body to relax.

Allow your toes and feet to relax. Enjoy the sense of calm as this feeling moves gently upward in your legs and into the pelvic area of your body.

Take another deep breath and, as you exhale, feel the calm energy now gently moving into the stomach region and then into your chest.

Take another deep breath and, this time as you exhale, allow this feeling of repose to move into your shoulders, and then down your arms, into your hands and into your fingers.

114

Now, sense the serenity moving from your shoulders, up the back of your neck to the top of your head, and then moving gently down the front of your face all the way to your chin.

Now feel the relaxation coming down from your shoulders, through your back and spinal column into your tailbone.

Your body and mind are filled with peaceful relaxation.

And now use your own personal method to allow yourself to go into an even deeper, more relaxed state of body and mind.

Choose your own particular way of going deeper.

Feel yourself going into a deeper, healthier level of consciousness.

It is a marvelous feeling to be relaxed!

And now there will be a countdown from 7 to 1 that will help you adjust to the appropriate level of consciousness for discovering your own personal key to the essence of letting go.

With each descending number you will go into a deeper, more-relaxed state of consciousness.

At the count of 1 you will be totally relaxed and completely at ease.

7 - 6 - 5. You are going down, down, down into a deeper, healthier level of consciousness.

4 - 3 - 2.

At the count of 1 you will imagine yourself on an ocean beach at sunrise. It is your own private beach, a place where you will be very safe and secure.

1.

The Journey Begins

Imagine yourself standing on a beach, facing the ocean at dawn. Look at and listen to the gentle, rhymthic waves as they make their way onto the shore.

Touch the smooth, soft sand with your hand.

Smell the fresh, still air.

You can taste the cool morning dew.

Feel with your heart the magic of early morning.

Now watch the brilliant, crimson sun as it rises from below the horizon, signaling the beginning of a new day. Look at the magnificent beauty of the sky as the darkness of night turns to the light of day.

You are alone on your own private beach. You feel secure. Sense the total safety of this beach.

Now turn to your left and see a winding path of sand before you.

As you get ready to begin your journey down the beach, allow the clothing you are wearing to fall to the ground. You are willing to go off freely to discover for yourself your own personal key to the essence of letting go.

You begin to walk, with your right foot first, then with your left.

As the beach winds to the left you notice a finely-meshed screen before you. It is slightly taller and wider than you, several inches thick. You understand that this screen symbolizes your self-pity.

The screen has been placed there to help you to filter out your self-pity.

Self-Pity

You could go around the screen but you consciously decide you want to liberate yourself from self-pity.

As you look at the screen, you begin to recognize what this self-pity honestly represents for you.

Is it that you feel sorry for yourself for not being fully appreciated for what you have done for others?

Does it occur when you allow yourself to be controlled by others, and then blame others for what is happening in your life?

Or does it happen when you control others because of your own weaknesses, since remaining in a state of self-pity can become very comfortable, or at least seem to be so?

Now you consciously decide you are willing to take full responsibility for your actions and the consequences of your actions. The more you can release self-pity, the more glorious your journey in life becomes.

Begin to walk slowly through the screen. Feel your self-pity peeling off of you: it sticks to the screen.

On the other side of the screen, you feel lighter and more free. You are detached from your self-pity.

Without looking back, continue your walk down the beach. As you turn left at another bend in the beach you see a similar screen in front of you. This one you understand to be the screen of your anger.

Anger

Again you could walk around the screen but you consciously choose to release the hidden anger you have harbored deep inside of you.

Which aspect of your experience of separation do you feel most angry about now?

Is it a particular experience which led you to feel angry; an experience which you have repressed because you didn't feel you had a right to be angry?

Is it a suppressed anger from an experience that seemed too minor to discuss at that time?

Or are you feeling anger that was caused by a sudden change in your life that was not positive?

Mentally bring forth the picture of that experience. How did you really want to respond at the time?

And now you decide to release yourself from your anger. Walk slowly through the screen.

Sense yourself becoming lighter as the screen strips away your anger.

On the other side of the screen, you feel liberated from your anger.

Without looking back, continue your walk down the beach. The beach winds slightly left again, this time into a small cove where you notice another screen before you. This is the screen of your shame.

Shame

As you stand before this screen, picture mentally the action — either words or deeds of other people — that caused you to have a feeling of shame about yourself.

Was the shame the result of an experience in the relationship with the person from whom you are now separating?

Is the feeling of shame related to something you were taught by family, religion, society or culture?

Did the action of others make you feel worthless?

And what is that shame doing to you now? How is it affecting your life now? Have you convinced yourself that you are defective or flawed?

Or is the shame related to an action in which you may have been the offender? Was there something you may have said or done that produced in another the feeling of shame?

And now you consciously decide to end the shame. You realize there is no action that is not forgivable.

And, with a deep sense of sincerity, you consciously decide to forgive yourself and others.

Walk slowly through the screen. As you step through the screen you will leave the shame behind. You are disengaging yourself from the shame.

On the other side of the screen, you experience a wondrous feeling of jubilation.

You are now more footloose as you leave the cove and continue your walk down the beach. You look ahead and before you is another screen. You have now arrived at the screen of your fear.

Fear

With increased self-confidence, consciously decide to confront one of your greatest fears.

Facing the screen, you picture that fear before you. What is that fear?

Is it a fear of loneliness? A fear of being outside the realm of love?

Is it a fear of the unknown? A fear of success, of failure, of responsibility?

And now look at what that fear has done to you. Has it kept you from being in touch with your feelings or your thoughts?

As you look at the screen you understand the basis of your fear and what it is a symptom of. You understand the belief that lies behind the fear, the belief that you need to change.

You forgive yourself for not having conquered your fear before now, and you give yourself permission to free yourself from your fear.

With the knowledge of what your fear is and what it is a symptom of, walk slowly through the screen. As you walk through the screen, you know that you have conquered your fear.

You now feel an even greater sense of freedom. Continue walking down the beach until you come upon another screen. You understand this is the screen of your pain.

Pain

You could choose to bypass this screen and go around it but you decide to confront your pain.

As you stand before the screen, you see the image of your pain and the impact it has had on you and others.

You decide to no longer mask, deny or ignore your pain.

Face your sorrows. Face the hopelessness. Face the helplessness. Face the despair.

Feel the love you want but know you will never have.

Feel the dreams you seek but know will never come true.

You made mistakes. You messed up. Your control, your manipulation, your hidden agendas have caused you and others pain. You feel so sorry and have so much remorse.

Let yourself feel the sorrow. Feel the hurt that is deep in your very bones.

Feel the loneliness. Feel the abandonment. Feel the alienation. Feel the feelings.

And when you feel there is no more then feel it again. Let the pain pour out of you.

Let out every bit of rage. Let out every bit of hate and bitterness, every bit of fury. Let it flow out of you.

And now with your strength of character and self-forgiveness you walk slowly through the screen feeling the last remnants of pain being stripped away from you.

You sense the pain sticking to the screen as you make your way to the other side.

You continue your walk down the beach, and as the beach winds to the left you come upon another screen. You understand that this is the screen of your freedom.

Freedom

As you stand before this screen you are now ready to relinquish the last limitation that has kept you from being totally free; and kept you tied to the past.

What is that obstacle for you?

Is it a feeling of not being worthy? A feeling that you don't love well enough and never will?

Is it rejection?

Is it the way in which you continue to punish yourself?

Is it the way in which you continue to sabotage yourself?

Is it a resentment that you hold?

Is it an area where you lack trust in yourself or in someone else?

Is it an addiction that you have?

Is it a faulty belief you have about yourself?

Is it a thought that keeps you tied to the past?

Create the picture with your mental eye.

Now give yourself permission to walk through the screen.

Step forward, with your right foot first.

As you walk slowly through the screen, you leave your limitations behind.

On the other side of the screen, you feel an exuberance, an aliveness that you have never felt before. And in a quiet whisper say: "I am free."

Continue down the beach and you will see the final screen.

The Essence

When you walk through this last screen, you will strip away all of your physical nature as you have known it until now, and what will remain on the other side of the screen will be the essence of who you are.

Stand before the screen willing to discover for yourself the key to letting go.

Walk through the screen. It is effortless.

Now you sense the essence of who you really are. This is for you a new dimension — of physical and spiritual reality combined.

Everything else is gone. All that remains is the essence of who you are.

You are that essence. This essence is your true reality.

What is this essence for you?

Picture this essence of your existence. Imagine its shape. Touch it. Hear it. Smell it. Taste it. Experience it.

You sense that this essence is connected to a Spiritual Power somewhere in the distance. The essence of who you are is a Spiritual gift.

What connects your essence to that Spiritual Power is an energy which you can sense, which you can feel, which you can know. Sense it. Feel it. Know it.

Now you realize that you are a part of that Spiritual Power.

Decide to receive more of the energy which connects you to that Spiritual Power.

And, through your willingness to receive more of the energy that connects you to the Spiritual Power, your entire being takes shape.

The energy has now become a part of your every organ, every gland, every cell, every drop of blood. It is a part of your every breath.

You are the energy and the essence.

Celebration

Turn slowly to the right and once again face the ocean, realizing that life is a gift and it is yours to embrace.

You notice that the beauty of day has turned into the magnificent wonder of night. Billions of stars fill the sky. The moon illuminates all you can see from where you stand.

With a new aliveness and freedom, and with gratitude to yourself and to your Spiritual Power, silently say "Thank You," and let the words flow over the ocean and beyond the horizon.

The gentle waves coming into the shore will bring you the reply. Listen.

You are filled with love and joy.

You are whole and complete and you begin to celebrate.

Start to laugh, a laughter that resonates throughout your body.

Picture yourself beginning to dance. Spread your arms. Twirl. Leap. Laugh. Dance your dance. Feel the celebration.

And now you notice a robe on the beach. Pick it up and wrap yourself in it. You feel wonderful.

You sense you are not alone. There is someone there with you. Someone who is always there for you. Who is it?

You feel wondrously calm and at peace.

You now turn to the left and see a wide beach path before you. Without looking back, face this path and your future.

Ahead of you is a world that is waiting for you, waiting for you to create its future. And you know you can create anything you want if you truly desire it. For you now have a greater Spiritual awareness of who you are.

You have a greater sense of self-love and self-worth.

The essence of who you are forms the basis of your self-forgiveness and your responsibility to yourself and others.

That essence is a part of the choices you make, your feelings and your thoughts. It is the foundation of your belief system.

You face the future with a greater self-confidence and trust in yourself.

Begin to walk forward. Begin to walk in love. To walk in love.

The Return

At the count of 5, gently open your eyes. You will be fully awake and fully alert. Feeling vibrantly alive.

You have discovered for yourself your own personal key to the art of letting go.

1 - 2 - 3 - 4 and 5. Eyes open. Wide awake. You are vibrantly alive.

This book was designed with two primary goals in mind: the growth of your self-knowledge and the development of your ability to act in a way that is beneficial to you. It is sincerely hoped that these goals have been met, that *The Art of Letting Go* has helped you to work through the difficulties of a breakup in a relationship. I welcome your comments and wish you well on your journey.

Carlino Giampolo

P.O. Box 15182, Honolulu, Hawaii 96830

The Art of Letting Go grew out of Carlino Giampolo's personal experiences. Having himself survived the breakup of several intimate relationships, he has now mapped out for others what he found to be an exciting and rewarding journey from pain to the joy of new beginnings.

Normally, books of this nature are written by psychiatrists or psychologists. Giampolo is neither of these. But he believes that the voice of an ordinary person, like himself, is just as important in helping people to understand themselves. His readers through the years agree wholeheartedly.

The Art of Letting Go has been used by professionals in workshops for people experiencing divorce or the breakup of an intimate relationship. The book has also been used by psychologists as an aid in counseling their patients when they experience a breakup in love.